Daring
To Hope

Daring To Hope

Sermons For Pentecost
(Last Third)
Cycle B First Lesson Texts

John P. Rossing

CSS Publishing Company, Inc.
Lima, Ohio

DARING TO HOPE

Copyright © 1993 by
The CSS Publishing Company, Inc.
Lima, Ohio

All rights reserved. No part of this publication may be reproduced, stored in a retrieval system, or transmitted in any form or by any means, electronic, mechanical, photocopying, recording, or otherwise, without the prior permission of the publisher. Inquiries should be addressed to: The CSS Publishing Company, Inc., 628 South Main Street, Lima, Ohio 45804.

Library of Congress Cataloging-in-Publication Data

Rossing, John P., 1956-
    Daring to hope : sermons for Pentecost (last third) first lesson, cycle B / by John P. Rossing.
        p.   cm.
    ISBN 1-55673-615-0
    1. Pentecost season — Sermons. 2. Sermons, American. 3. Bible. O.T. — Sermons. I. Title.
    BV61.R68   1993
    252'.6—dc20   92-2759
                                                                                                 CIP

9340 / ISBN 1-55673-615-0   PRINTED IN U.S.A.

To Matt Ernst

and

to the members of
All Saints Lutheran Church in Lilburn

Table Of Contents

Introduction   9

Proper 22   11
It Just Isn't Fair
Job 1:1, 2:1-10

Proper 23   17
Bold Talk Of Faith
Job 23:1-9, 16-17

Proper 24   23
"Because I'm God"
Job 38:1-7 (34-41)

Proper 25   29
Daring To Hope
Job 42:1-6, 10-17

Proper 26   35
A Faith, A Farm And A Family
Ruth 1:1-18

Proper 27   41
God's Way Of Doing Things
Ruth 3:1-5; 4:13-17

Proper 28   47
Hope For The Barren
1 Samuel 1:4-20

All Saints' Sunday 53
   What Do We Hope For?
   Isaiah 25:6-9

Christ The King 59
   The King And The Covenant
   2 Samuel 23:1-7

Thanksgiving Day 65
   Bugs
   Joel 2:21-27

Notes 71

Lectionary Preaching After Pentecost 73

Introduction

"Hope is the margin of difference."

So said the Reverend James Alexander Forbes, Jr., senior minister at the Riverside Church in New York City. Forbes was preaching in Ebenezer Baptist Church in Atlanta, at the 1992 worship service for the Martin Luther King, Jr. holiday. Speaking of people in our nation who are poor, homeless, unemployed or neglected by their families and society, he said there is one important reason why some keep trying to succeed within the system while others turn to drugs, crime, idleness and other destructive behaviors: some people still hope for a better future, others have stopped hoping. The violence that erupted in Los Angeles, Atlanta and other cities only a few weeks later seemed to confirm Forbes' words; when hope for change dies, people's only response to despair is violent rage.

Hope is the margin of difference. In suburban and rural churches as well as in urban neighborhoods, people can bear life's burdens only if they believe their suffering will be relieved. At a recent discussion attended by a group of Lutheran pastors, one participant said, "Our parishioners need to hear a message of hope. The messages they hear from the news media, from politicians and from our culture are too often messages of fear. Most people seem to go through life guided by their fear of doing the wrong thing rather than by any hope of fulfillment."

In the final weeks of the church year our attention turns toward that very hope of fulfillment. The lessons begin to sound eschatological themes, guiding the church toward the destination God has planned for it. The Old Testament readings that make up the first lessons for the last third of the Pentecost season repeatedly tell stories of hope, of people whose despair is transformed into trust in God's providence.

While the eschatological note is heard, especially in the readings for All Saints' and Christ the King Sundays, the hope is not all other-worldly. The stories of Job, Ruth and Hannah show us ordinary people experiencing deliverance from grief, loss, poverty and alienation through God's acts on their behalf. Yet neither is the hope unrealistic or too worldly. Job and Hannah, for example, derive their hope from learning that God still cares for them; such a hope can sustain people even when their physical circumstances remain difficult.

Faith, hope and love are the abiding attributes of the Christian life. Most of us proclaim faith and love consistently, and theology and ethics make up the two great intellectual enterprises of the church. But if the pastor in the discussion group was right, and if James Forbes interpreted our social problems correctly, we may be guilty of neglecting the third great gift God has given us. During the closing Sundays of the church year we have an opportunity to declare our hope boldly.

Proper 22
Job 1:1, 2:1-10

It Just Isn't Fair

Job is a fascinating book. It's a literary masterpiece, a collection of poetic discussions about faith, suffering, God's justice, the human mind. The occasion for these discussions is the story of Job, a wealthy and important man who is devoutly religious, scrupulously moral and careful of everything he says and does, yet who loses everything in his life because of a whimsical argument between God and Satan.

Most of us remember Job for his patience, but the patient sufferer who accepts his ill fortune as God's will without complaining only appears in this opening story. In the rest of the book Job is shown arguing his innocence, rejecting his friends' efforts to counsel him, searching for explanations, challenging God's justice. Today and for the next three Sundays we'll be looking at Job's experiences and reaction to them, and in Job's struggle to preserve his faith in spite of his tragedy, we can find echoes of the questions many of us ask when we or people we know suffer unexpectedly, unfairly or unexplainably.

Today our text is the opening story, in which the big issue seems to be fairness. Fairness is an indispensable doctrine, basic to life in human society. We demand fair taxes, fair judges, fair housing, fair labor contracts, fair fights. Children learn to play fair, and one of their favorite arguments against something their parents have decided is "it's not fair." Fairness simply stated is this: you get treated the way you deserve to get treated, and everyone who deserves the same gets the same.

And the first thing we notice about the book of Job is the unfairness. Job is good, religious, careful, intelligent, devoted to his family; and his virtue and wisdom have made him wealthy, successful and respected. Job is so good, in fact, that God starts to brag about him. God's high opinion of Job rouses Satan's interest, and Satan proposes to test the sincerity of Job's faith. He clobbers Job with tragedy upon tragedy. Job loses his herds and his servants, then all his children are killed in a freak storm. In today's reading Job's health turns bad and he begins to suffer disfigurement and physical pain on top of his sorrow.

It's not fair. A good man like Job shouldn't suffer like that. But we're used to that kind of unfairness. A young woman shouldn't get AIDS from her dentist, nor should a baby get AIDS from its mother. Honest, hard-working people shouldn't lose their homes and have to live on the street. Good people's marriages shouldn't fail. Little children shouldn't get killed in drive-by shootings. Innocent people shouldn't die in wars, or be killed by drunk drivers. Nobody should get cancer or multiple sclerosis, or Alzheimer's disease.

So the story of Job sounds true to us. It offends our sense of justice; it violates our standard of reward for virtue and punishment for vice; it puts God in the questionable position of allowing Job to suffer — but it sounds true. Life shoves unfairness in our faces every day. And if Job's story sounds like stories we know, then maybe the lessons we can learn from Job can help us survive the suffering in our own lives.

The first of those lessons is this: religion isn't the key to prosperity, health or success. People have thought it was since long before Job's day, and still do. God rewards the good and faithful with good things in life. That kind of thinking makes our faithfulness part of a bargain with God: if we believe, worship and obey God, then God is somehow obligated to bless us with good things.

And from there it's an easy step to being religious mainly for the goodies. Television ministers are notorious for that sort of thing: "Be faithful, tune in to my show and give generously to support my ministry and I guarantee God will bless you materially and spiritually." Faith healers, too: "If you really believe, God will grant your miracle." *Consumer's Research* magazine has even published an article warning people about the boom in religious swindlers, who promise incredible returns on investments in religious scams.[1]

But it isn't only swindlers who look at faith that way. Most of us do. In our preaching and proclamation we try to motivate faith by promising rewards: Believe in Jesus so you will go to heaven when you die. That isn't the way Jesus made the invitation. When Jesus called his disciples he didn't say, "Follow me if you want to be a winner," or "Follow me; I'll get you into heaven." He said, "Follow me." (Mark 2:14) Later, he said, "Take up your cross and follow me," (Mark 8:34) and "give all that you have to the poor and follow me." (Mark 10:21) As Dietrich Bonhoeffer wrote, "When Christ calls [us] he bids [us] come and die."[2] Jesus didn't ask people to follow him for the good they'd get out of it, but because he wanted them in his kingdom.

That's the point at which Satan thought Job was vulnerable. He bet God that Job was only faithful because it brought him prosperity, and that if the reward went away so would Job's faith. But Job proved him wrong. The first thing we learn from Job's story is that faithfulness to God is not a guarantee of a sorrow-free life. A faith that depends on the promise of rewards is likely to fail us when suffering comes.

Now, the flip side of the idea that happiness is a reward for virtue is that suffering is a punishment for sin. Even if we know intellectually that it's not, we still find it emotionally comforting to find some way to blame people for their own suffering. It's convenient to think of AIDS as the consequence of behaviors that people should have known better than to engage in. One pastor has spoken of walking into a hospital room to visit a smoker dying of lung cancer and having to force himself to feel sympathetic because, after all, he was asking for it, wasn't he? People we see in shelters for homeless families must have messed up somehow to have lost their homes. The high incidence of crime and drug use among young black men must have something to do with bad character, or bad parents, or bad something.

That kind of thinking helps us deal with suffering. It makes it a little less threatening if we can explain it, or blame someone for it. If people suffer because of something they've done, then if we avoid doing the same thing we can avoid suffering. It also clears us of any guilt and, more important, it clears God of any responsibility.

The only problem is that it's wrong. Job shows us that. Job was entirely blameless, entirely faultless, yet he suffered horribly. His story confronts us with the problem we'd like to avoid, innocent suffering. Recently a young man who had just graduated from Emory University in Atlanta — a 21-year-old All-American swimmer, strong, healthy and admired by everyone who knew him — dropped dead of a heart attack while sitting and watching television with his girlfriend. How do you account for something like that? You don't, that's the problem. None of the usual explanations work. It just isn't fair.

Someone said once in a Sunday school class that the things we fear the most are those we can't understand and those we can't control, and suffering often falls into both those categories. Does this story offer us any solutions?

No, it doesn't appear to. Job's story doesn't help us understand why we suffer. The story about God and Satan making a gentlemen's bet on whether Job would stay faithful doesn't really explain anything. In fact, it doesn't appear plausible at all. The picture of God sitting around with a few close personal friends — including Satan — swapping opinions about human beings doesn't square with any other information in the Bible, so most commentators take this to be an ancient folk tale that the author of Job used as the setting for his reflections on suffering. In other words, it doesn't really give us reliable information about why tragedy befalls Job, or us.

That's just like God, isn't it, to leave us in the dark about important things. Martin Luther wrote of the *deus absconditus,* the hidden God, by which he meant that God has chosen to reveal some things about himself — particularly his gift of salvation through his Son Jesus — but has chosen not to reveal other things. And why there is suffering in the world is one of them. When Moses went up on the mountain to meet God, all God would let Moses see was his backside, and that's all he shows us; we just aren't meant to know everything about God's ways. (Exodus 33:23)

Nor does this story give us control over suffering. It doesn't help us anticipate it or cure it. Job's wife tells him he could end his suffering if he would curse God and get zapped by lightning — you might say she wrote the first suicide manual — but Job refuses.

Yet that does not mean that suffering is out of control. We can't control it, but the story of Job suggests to us that God is in control. Satan can't afflict Job without God's permission or beyond limits set by God. Job observes, in the last verse of today's text, that both the good and the evil he received in life were from God. And because Job believes God to be trustworthy, he is willing to submit to God's decision. We might not know why God allows us to suffer, or refrains from intervening on our behalf, but we can believe that God knows what he is doing. God is in control of suffering as well as salvation; and he proved to us in the death and resurrection of Jesus that he will not run away from suffering, but also that suffering can be redeemed and even redemptive.

Maybe that makes us want to cry out to our heavenly Father, "It isn't fair." But when human parents make decisions that their children think are unfair, they usually have good reasons that their children simply can't understand. Still, they hope their children will trust them enough to accept their decisions. The picture we get in today's story of God and Job is like that. Job can't understand why he has to suffer, any more than we can when we read about him, but he trusts God to do the right thing. That kind of faith might not end our suffering, but it allows us to survive.

Proper 23
Job 23:1-9, 16-17

Bold Talk
Of Faith

One of Gary Larson's *The Far Side* cartoons is called "God at his computer." It shows God with long white hair and beard watching a computer screen where an unlucky-looking fellow is walking down a sidewalk with a piano suspended by a cable over his head. God's hand is on the computer keyboard, and his finger is hovering over a key labeled "SMITE."³

The cartoon suggests two things about God's way of determining a person's fate: first, that God is impersonal and inaccessible. God with his finger on the smite key is no more personally involved with the man whose fate he's deciding than a child playing video games is with the Super Mario Brothers. Second, God appears arbitrary and capricious: "Shall I smite this guy or spare him? What kind of a mood am I in today?"

Our first look at Job may have left us with the same impressions about God. He's distant, unconcerned, playing games with Job's life and fortunes just to see what happens. But today's lesson challenges those impressions. In chapter 23 we see that Job doesn't believe God is either impersonal or arbitrary.

Of course, Job has every reason to think God is remote and aloof. "Oh, that I knew where I might find him, that I might come even to his dwelling!" Job cries. God appears to have moved and left no forwarding address. In chapter one,

Job knew where to find God: He prayed and made all the required burnt-offerings, confident that God was listening and responding the way he was supposed to. But now Job wonders whether he had been naive to think God was listening, or whether God has broken faith with him.

It's a common complaint of people who suffer: "My God, my God, why have you forsaken me?" The writer of Psalm 22 and Jesus on the cross both felt as though God had turned his back on them. Elie Wiesel, the Nobel Prize-winning author and concentration camp survivor, has written of how Jews in World War II often felt that God had abandoned them.

Job felt that way, too. "Where is God in my suffering? I can't find him in front of me or behind me, on my left or on my right." But Job wouldn't settle for that. Despite appearances to the contrary, despite feeling as though God had left him alone in deep darkness, Job believed that God was there; Job was confident that God was approachable. God wasn't like a kid playing video games, or like the Wicked Witch of the West watching Dorothy in her crystal ball. Job believed he could talk to God about his problem and God would hear him.

"Even when God is silent," Job seems to have thought, "even when God is hidden, we can depend on our relationship with him." Martin Luther once said, speaking of the Bible's assurance that God hears our prayers, "If it weren't for the promise I wouldn't pray."[4] That might have been Job's motto: "If it weren't for the promise I wouldn't pray." Job, too, trusted that God would not break faith with anyone who called out to him.

Job not only believed that God was approachable, he wanted to see him. One might have expected him to turn his back on God, the way it seemed God had turned his back on Job. I'm sure we all know neighbors or family members who haven't spoken to each other in years out of indignation over some injustice or hurt feelings. You may also know people who don't believe in God any more because God let their child die, or their business fail. That's just what Satan was hoping

Job would do when he proposed his test. Satan suspected that once the material advantage of faith in God was lost, Job would want nothing more to do with God.

But he was wrong. Instead of swearing off religion once God let him down, Job went looking for God. Job wouldn't let his relationship with God die. When a friend or relative or spouse has hurt your feelings, you can walk away from the relationship, or you can go to the person at fault and raise the issue with them in hopes of solving the problem. The first alternative might save your pride and preserve your indignation, but the second might save the friendship or the marriage. Job chose the second alternative when he didn't feel like God had treated him fairly. "God," he said, "I need to talk to you."

In fact, what Job really said was "God, I demand to talk with you." This isn't the same Job we saw in chapters one and two, the patient sufferer willing to accept both good and evil from God. "If I could find God," Job said, "I would lay my case before him and fill my mouth with arguments." That's bold talk. That's audacity. That even sounds sinful, for Job to argue with God and announce that he can force God to change his mind, doesn't it?

I recently heard a story of a retired pastor, a faithful, devout and humble man. Around Easter one year his wife, who was several years younger than he, was taken ill, and by the end of the summer she was dead. He was devastated. He grieved inconsolably for months; a year later he would still burst into sobbing tears several times a day. His family began to fear for his mental health. He was utterly unable to accept his wife's death. He often admitted that he was tempted to be angry with God, to ask why God would have taken his wife from him, but he didn't dare. He obviously was angry with God; he did want to know why. But he didn't believe he was allowed to feel that way, and his hidden anger and confusion ate up his soul like acid.

Job didn't have such scruples about giving God a piece of his mind. He was angry, and he believed that it was best to get his complaint out in the open. It didn't seem to matter to Job whether he was acting in a proper, God-fearing manner or not. He was simply being honest about the way he felt.

One student in a college Bible survey class was offended that Job would challenge and argue with God. "What did Job think gave him the right to talk to God that way?" she asked. Another student spoke up and said, "Faith. Job trusted God enough that he knew God wouldn't turn against him even if he lost his temper. If you really love someone," she went on, "and know that they love you, you don't have to be afraid to let them know when you're unhappy."

Job's faith is evident in ironic ways throughout this chapter. Far from being signs of lack of faith, his anger with God and his desire to confront God and argue his case before God actually show how firmly he believed God had entered into a relationship with his people that allowed them access to God.

The second idea about God that Job rejected in this passage was that God is arbitrary or unfair. Job was convinced that God is just, and if he could prove to God that he was innocent his suffering would end. Job couldn't believe God would ever let an innocent man suffer and he expected to win a reprieve if he could get a hearing in God's court.

Job is crawling out on a mighty skinny limb here. The idea that innocent people don't suffer and guilty ones do is exactly what the opening of Job's story cautioned against believing. There is no necessary connection between suffering and guilt. So, is this story trying to tell us God plays games with our fate, or that we can't expect fair play from God? No, but in a world deeply immersed in sin and torn apart by the conflict between good and evil, there is no simple way to define a category like fairness.

By late Old Testament times the people of Israel were starting to realize that. The author of Job, along with the writer of some latter parts of Isaiah, began to think about the problem of innocent suffering. Job found it vexing, while Isaiah found it revealing, even redemptive. In the New Testament we see the idea of fairness come completely unbuckled when God puts innocence itself to death on the cross in the person of his Son Jesus.

But Job didn't understand that yet. He knew how he expected God to act, and couldn't imagine that God would have standards different from his own. Job didn't realize that God exists and acts far beyond the realm of human judgment. We can't look at God's actions and call them fair or unfair, or right or wrong. God is sovereign, God is absolute, God answers to no authority or standards of justice but his own.

And Job's reliance on his own judgment caused him another problem. His claim to righteousness was based completely on his good works. He had done right, he hadn't done wrong, therefore God owed him a judgment in his favor. But as Paul wrote in Romans (3:20, 23), no one can make that claim. By virtue of being members of a sinful humanity we are all guilty before God, whether we've broken any rules or not. If God were to be completely fair with us we would all suffer condemnation. It's only by God's mercy that we receive any blessings at all, for we certainly don't deserve them.

So when Job suggested that God hadn't been fair with him, he unwittingly made another confession of faith. God doesn't deal with us as we deserve, but as he chooses. God doesn't give us what he owes, but what he wants to give us. One commentator on Job wrote, "The questioner scans the heavens and finds the supposed throne of mercy without an occupant."[5] But I don't think that's Job's problem. Job isn't looking for God in the throne of mercy, but in the throne of justice. That's the throne that's empty. Job is looking for the wrong thing from God.

Job never asked God for mercy, or help, or love, or grace, only for a verdict. Yet even though Job may have asked the wrong questions of God, and made the wrong assumption about how God acted, at least he asked. His challenge to God was the real mark of Job's faith. He never doubted that God was there, that God was in control of the situation, or that God listened and responded to human cries.

We experience the same doubts, the same nagging absences of God that Job did. But we have some advantages. We know that God came into the world to redeem suffering through the suffering of his Son. We know that God has restored us to life by grace, not justice. And when we don't seem to be able to find God anywhere he shows himself to us in the preaching of his Word, in the waters of baptism, in bread and wine. His presence among us in word and sacrament proves that he is neither distant nor uncaring.

Proper 24
Job 38:1-7 (34-41)

"Because I'm God"

A mother is running errands, accompanied by her two small children. All morning the children have been pestering her: "Can we go to the new toy store? Let's get some ice cream. We want to go home now." Pretty soon their pestering turns to complaining, then to angry questions. "Why can't we go where we want to go? Why do we have to go in that store? Why can't we eat lunch now? Why do we always have to do what you want to do and never what we want to do?" Finally the mother stops, stoops to face her children chin-to-chin and says, "Because I'm the Mommy, that's why."

That scenario reminds me of the way God responds to Job in this morning's lesson. Job has progressed from acceptance of his suffering to complaining to questioning to bitter accusations. Now at the climax of the book God finally speaks to Job and his answer is, "Because I'm God, that's why."

It's surprising that God appears to Job at all here. God hasn't spoken since he gave Satan permission to test Job's faith in the opening scene of the book, and he has never spoken directly to Job. Job has been frustrated by God's silence. He has hoped, even demanded, to argue his case before God; he has pressed God for answers, but he has gotten no response. Perhaps God has simply been exercising patience with Job, letting Job blow off steam. But, on the other hand, maybe

God has disappeared from the story. In last week's lesson, Job was stymied by his inability to figure out where God was when he wanted to talk to God. Now, suddenly, with no preparation or introduction, the voice of God roars out of the whirlwind.

Why does God speak now, when he has been silent so long? Not because Job talked him into it; not because he figured he owed it to Job. God hasn't placed himself under obligation to Job at any point in the story. No, God speaks now only because he chooses this moment to speak. In fact, it's only by God's choice that he speaks at all in the Bible. God reveals to human beings only what he wishes us to know, and only when he chooses to reveal it. Many times we pray and plead, and then wait endlessly for an answer from God. But God won't be coerced into acting.

Not only does God not appear to Job on demand; when he does speak he doesn't answer any of Job's questions. Job wanted God to appear and explain his actions, defend the justice of what he has allowed to happen to Job. Job wanted God to answer Job's accusations. Instead, God appears and begins questioning Job.

"Who is this that darkens counsel by words without knowledge?" God demands. "Who are you, to tell me I don't know how to run the world?" Then God gets sarcastic. "Let's check out your qualifications to criticize me. I assume, since you think you know better than I do how to create a universe, that you have some relevant experience. What was your role in creation? Do you recall the blueprints, the measurements? Refresh my memory — were you the design engineer or the construction supervisor?"

Of course, Job can only stand silently. He's been had, and he knows it. It's immediately plain that he has neither any expertise nor authority that allows him to challenge God. God has used another technique that parents often use to squelch complaints from their children. "You don't like what I made for supper? Fine, I'm sure tomorrow night you can cook something you'd like better. You didn't enjoy our vacation? Sorry, next time we'll let you make the plans and pay the bills."

God doesn't think he owes Job an explanation. So instead of answering Job's questions, he simply asserts his authority. "Can you send forth lightnings, that they may go and say to you, 'Here we are!'?" he asks Job. "Can you make rain, or food for lions?" God's question implies its own answer, of course: "No, you can't; but I can, because I'm God."

Ironically, early in the book Job had told his friends that he couldn't really argue with God, because it would be no contest. In chapter nine — 29 chapters ago — Job said, "If I summoned him and he answered me, I do not believe that he would listen to my voice. ... If it is a contest of strength, he is the strong one." (9:16, 19) Now God proves that Job was right. He shows up and crushes Job's arguments with his power and authority.

So Job gets what he wanted, in a way. God finally appears and speaks to him, just as Job has been demanding. But the result is not a victory for Job. It's not even a fair fight. Instead, God comes and teaches Job a harsh lesson. Job's opinions have outpaced his understanding; he has set himself up as judge of things he has no competence to judge. Job has been playing God, and when God shows up Job's game is ended.

In ancient drama, when a writer wrote such a complicated plot he couldn't come up with a way to resolve it, he might have a divine being lowered from the stage rafters by a crane to work a miracle and make everything right again. That technique was called *deus ex machina,* "God from a machine." We often think of God that way, as the one who is hanging in the rafters, waiting to swoop down and solve our problems for us when we really need him. Job may have thought the same thing. God was bound to come when Job called and straighten out Job's affairs; that was his job.

But God didn't come when Job called. God waited, and Job waited, and God finally came when he decided it was time to come. And when God came, it wasn't to answer Job's questions but to put Job in his place. God came and reminded Job that he — God — was the one who designed and created the earth, and no one is competent or authorized to judge him.

We, like Job, must remember that although God has promised to answer our prayers and to act on our behalf, it is only because he chooses to. God doesn't take orders from us or defend himself to us.

Well, all of that doesn't present a very flattering picture of God, does it? God keeps people waiting, and then when he does reply to their cries it's to pull rank or to make fun of their complaints. So is God a tyrant? Perhaps, but this passage reminds us that if God is the absolute ruler of the world it's because he is its designer, creator, provider and sustainer. Returning to the analogy of parents, God is like a parent who tells his children, "As long as I provide the roof over your head, the clothes on your back and the food on your plate, I will also make the rules, and decide what's fair."

Besides, if God is a dictator, he's a benevolent one. After all, he may be slow to respond, and his response may not be what we want to hear, but he does respond. He answers Job, which shows that he has been listening and watching all along. From the beginning, Job's ordeal has been a test of his faith, and he has passed; he has never given up on God. Now, at the end, God vindicates Job's faith. He doesn't restore Job's fortune and reputation, but he does more than that. He comes in person to talk to Job, to show Job his glory. It's as if a peasant wrote to a king for a legal judgment, and instead of granting the judgment the king came to visit the peasant's house. What more could he ask for?

God proved his grace in this episode. He didn't have to listen to Job, or speak to him, but he did, because he chose to. Later, in a much more dramatic event, God initiated another unexpected contact with human beings when he became flesh in Jesus. He didn't have to come into the world to save us, but he did, because he chose to. He does the same for you and me this morning in the reading of his word, and in his presence in bread and wine. God doesn't have to hear our prayers, or speak to us, or come to us, but he does, because he cares.

We can also take comfort in what God reveals to Job about his control of the universe. In our text today and for the next two chapters, God reminds Job of all the things he has created, all the things that operate according to his design. The sun and the stars, the clouds and the rain, the animals, light and dark, the birth of baby mountain goats, the pride of a stallion — "I caused all that!" says God. He recites this long list mainly to show Job that he shouldn't try to tell God how to run his universe, but at the same time he points out to Job the pattern, the harmony, the orderliness, the appropriateness of things.

Does the sun do what it's supposed to? Does the rain do what it's supposed to? Does the snow fall when it's supposed to? Do lions eat what they're supposed to? Does it get dark when it's supposed to, and light when it's supposed to? The beauty, precision and harmony of creation should prove to us that God is the best creator of universes in the whole universe, so we can trust God to take care of us the way he's supposed to.

"Because I'm the Mommy, that's why" means, on the one hand, "I'm in charge here; I don't owe you any explanations; and you wouldn't understand if I did explain everything I do." But it also means, "I am your Mommy, I'm here with you, I know what I'm doing and you can trust me to look out for your best interests." God tells Job, "Because I'm God, that's why." He shows us the tremendous gap between our rights and his authority, between our speculation and his knowledge, between our dependence and his power. But at the same time he lays a foundation for trust: He is listening to us, he is present with us, and he is ruling the world with our interests at heart.

Proper 25
Job 42:1-6, 10-17

Daring To Hope

Last time we checked in with Job, God had just dropped a bombshell. After all Job's pleading, demanding and waiting, God had finally spoken to him and what God said had stunned Job. "You are in no position to accuse me, to question me, or to make demands of me," God said. "I'm in charge of the world, and accountable only to myself. You don't know the time of day when it comes to how the world is supposed to be run." And while God's answer put Job in his place, it also reassured him a bit, because God reminded Job of all sorts of evidence that God does know what he is doing. Besides, Job finally found out without a doubt that God was there with him and was listening to him.

The story could have ended right there. The message of the book had been delivered, Job had seen the big picture, and Satan's question had been answered. Job didn't lose faith even when his faith didn't protect him from suffering.

But the story didn't end after last week's lesson. Today we read what Paul Harvey would call "the rest of the story." There's an epilogue, a resolution to the story, in which some loose ends get tied up, and in which some of the biggest surprises in the book are still waiting for us.

First, we read about Job's reaction to the tongue-lashing he got from God. He is appropriately humbled. "You're right

God, and now I know it. I've been a fool, talking about things I didn't know anything about, thinking I understood mysteries way beyond me.'' Adam and Eve's first sin in the Garden of Eden, before they ever disobeyed God, was wanting to know what God knows, refusing to accept a dependent status. And Paul wrote in the New Testament that the first step in our salvation was for Jesus to give up his equality with God and be humbled, like the rest of us. Job's confession is our confession: We are not like God, and reaching for God-like understanding makes us fall.

But after Job confesses his sin, he confesses his faith. "I had heard of you by the hearing of the ear, but now my eye sees you." Now he knows that God is with him, because God has shown himself to Job. Before, he knew about God; now he knows God. Job didn't get the answers he wanted, but he got something much better. He got God himself.

You and I receive that same gift. Maybe God doesn't show himself to us visually like he did to Abraham and Moses and Job, but he shows himself to the world in Jesus. "Whoever has seen me has seen the Father," Jesus said; and we see Jesus right now, in his body the church, in the bread and wine of the sacrament, in the word that we read and preach. God is present with us just as surely as he was with Job, and because of God-with-us we can be full of hope and assurance.

After Job's confession, though, the lesson goes on, and it takes a surprising twist. Job's claims have been canceled; Job has withdrawn his demand for a reversal and has accepted God's gracious presence as a better hope than mere relief from suffering; and then God gives everything back to Job! He gives him twice as much as before — wealth, health, land, sons and daughters, respect and long life.

Why in the world would he do that? It's taken 40 chapters for this book to ease us away from the expectation of worldly blessings. We've finally learned that God's presence is the object of our faith, not the good things we might want from God. Now God makes everything the way it was before. Doesn't that ruin the whole story?

Our first thought might be that the ending makes the story unrealistic. It's like a fairy tale, where the hero lives happily ever after. We like to read Cinderella and Jack-and-the-Beanstalk and dream about fairy-tale scenes in our own lives, but we know it won't ever happen to us. It's the same way with Job. All the things he learned about patient suffering and appreciating God's presence don't mean much anymore when he's rich and happy again, do they? And what's the message for those of us who get sick and don't get well, who lose the farm and don't get it back, who lose a child and don't get two more twice as precious? "Sure, Job submitted to God's will, and it turned out that God's will was for him to drown in happiness. What good does that do me?"

For one thing, Job didn't know God was going to restore his fortunes when he repented of his arrogance and confessed his faith in God's presence. It wasn't the hope that he would get everything back that made him secure, it was that God would be with him wherever his journey took him. I suppose that when Job's life began to turn around he was as surprised as we are when we read about it. His faith didn't depend on prosperity or rewards any more.

So, then, what does the big reversal tell us? It tells us that suffering isn't forever. God cares and delivers us from suffering, just as he finally relieved Job's suffering. But we have to remember that in Job's day people didn't know anything about life after death. Suffering that wasn't relieved by the time a person died simply wasn't relieved, they thought. So if Job was to see deliverance it had to be in this life, in some kind of reversal of fortunes.

You and I have more possibilities than that. Because we have been promised the resurrection that Jesus first experienced, we believe that even suffering that dogs us to the grave will be replaced by joy, and by life without pain. Only it might happen after suffering has done its worst to us in death.

This turn of the story also tells us that God's gifts are unexpected and undeserved. God didn't have to give Job back his health, his family and his goods after all that had happened between him and Job. Job didn't expect it or need it anymore. But that's exactly why he did it. God doesn't bless us because he owes it to us, or because we insist on it. What we expect him to do he doesn't, and then he does what we don't expect him to, just because he wants to.

In an earlier sermon I said that Job was looking for justice from God, when he should have been asking for mercy. Justice is getting what you deserve, mercy is getting what you don't deserve, and what Job experiences here is a huge sample of God's mercy.

There is one surprise left in the story, and it might be the biggest one of all: Job starts his life over. He settles back down with his wife, has more children, takes up farming again. After all the pain he has felt, all the loss he has suffered, all the grief he has borne, he does it all over again, even though he risks suffering again.

Gregory of Nyssa, an early Christian theologian and monk, recommended the monastic life not because being celibate and removed from the world was any holier than being married and raising a family, but because it saved a person from the terrible pain of having loved ones and then losing them. Job knew the pain like few others have ever known it, and given a second chance he didn't choose to avoid the risk. He plunged back into family and friends and farming, knowing that he could lose it all again.

Archibald MacLeish wrote a play based on the story of Job a few years after World War II, called *J.B.* Two theater workers pretend that they're playing the roles of God and Satan on stage while they watch and comment on the story of Job. At the end, when Mr. Zuss, the God-character, tells Nickles, the Satan-character, that Job gets his life back and lives it over again, Nickles blows his stack:

> *Live his life again?*
> *Not even the most ignorant, obstinate,*
> *Stupid or degraded man*
> *This filthy planet ever farrowed,*

> *Offered the opportunity to live*
> *His bodily life twice over, would accept it —*
> *Least of all Job, ...*
> *It can't be borne twice over! Can't be!*

To which Mr. Zuss answers,

> *It is though. Time and again it is —*
> *Every blessed generation.*[6]

I think MacLeish was trying to say that the world could start life over again in the ashes of the War, in the nuclear age and the Cold War; that every generation makes a fresh start even though the pain and the suffering never go away.

What is it that allows "every blessed generation" to live with war and pain and disease and death and suffering? What is it that allows any of us to go on living when we've known loss, or sickness, or fear? It's the same thing that made Job dare to start over; it's hope.

Hope that bad things won't happen to us? No. Hope that we'll always get well when we're sick? No. Hope that we'll never have to spend a day hungry? No, though God may bless us in those ways, too. But Job's hope was that wherever his life led him he would be carried along by God's mercy.

We bring our children into the church through baptism when they're small and helpless. Every blessed generation does it. What makes parents think they haven't just brought another poor, suffering soul into a world of misery, that they haven't simply multiplied the world's heartache and their own? It's hope — hope that whatever joys or sorrows lie ahead for each child of God, we can depend on God to be faithful, to see us through. Without that hope, none of us could go on; daring to hope is everything.

Proper 26
Ruth 1:1-18

A Faith, A Farm
And A Family

John Denver wrote a song 20 years ago about wanting to get away from the big city to a place in the country — "somewhere to build me a faith, a farm and a family."[7] The story of Ruth reminds me of that song, because it's about simple people living on the land, and about the strength they draw from faith and family.

The story starts by telling us it took place "in the days when the judges ruled." Those were days of dreadful battles between God's people and their enemies, of mighty warriors and great heroes like Samson and Gideon and Deborah. But while mighty giants and epic events were changing the biblical world, people were still going about their regular lives trying to raise their crops and make a living; marrying, raising their children, mourning their dead. And those are the people and events the book of Ruth is about — everyday people leading everyday lives of love and hardship and hope.

We're accustomed to looking for God's work in dramatic events: in miracles like parting the Red Sea or changing water into wine, in sudden conversions, in the resurrection of the dead. But there aren't any apparent miracles in Ruth, no angel choirs, no revelations, no resurrections. Instead, this book reminds us that God also works in steady, unspectacular ways. Ruth is all about the quiet, constant, gentle providence of God — about things like a faith, a farm and a family.

First a farm. The book of Ruth is about farming folks trying to get a living from the land. In the first verse Naomi and her husband and sons leave Bethlehem because of a crop failure, hoping to do better in Moab. When Naomi decides to go back home, it's because God has "considered his people and given them food." Naomi and Ruth, the two widows, arrive back in Bethlehem at the time of the barley harvest, and Naomi sends Ruth out to glean in the fields so the two of them will have food. There in the barley field Ruth catches the eye of Boaz, her future husband. She romances him at the threshing place; he marries her and inherits Naomi's late husband's family farm, which becomes part of the family legacy of King David (and eventually of Jesus).

So farming, in this story, is part of a system of relations and operations that sustains people. It includes raising crops, but it also includes providing work and food for the two widows, finding a new husband and a home for Ruth, and passing a heritage from generation to generation. All those things, the story tells us, are in God's hands.

Farming, in this story, stands for the same things that "daily bread" stands for in the Lord's Prayer. Martin Luther, in his *Small Catechism*, wrote that when we pray for our daily bread we are asking God for "food and clothing, home and property, work and income, a devoted family, an orderly community, good government, favorable weather, peace and health, a good name and true friends and neighbors."[8] There's nothing we need in life that isn't part of God's gift to us through the normal processes of his creation. God is faithful to his people in the things that bring us salvation, but also in the things that bring us joy and comfort, from the food on our tables to our jobs, our spouses and our children.

The most obvious blessing in that array of gifts from God is family, and Ruth is probably best known as a family story. Naomi moves to Moab with her husband and two sons. Her two sons marry Moabite women, after which all three men die. One of her daughters-in-law, Ruth, returns to Bethlehem with Naomi as her loyal companion. Ruth works to support Naomi, while Naomi tries to find Ruth a new husband. A bachelor relative named Boaz falls in love with Ruth, marries her and begins a new family. It's a touching story of love and loyalty, and Ruth's pledge of faithfulness to Naomi, near the end of today's lesson, might be the most popular text in the Bible for weddings.

Naomi and her daughters-in-law were in a desperate situation at the beginning of this story. Women in their world had no status and no economic power except through their husbands and sons. Widows were powerless, and widows with no sons starved. So a household of three widows was the picture of hopelessness. Naomi had no options. She was too old to remarry and resigned herself to a life of poverty and loneliness. Her daughters-in-law, on the other hand, had a way out. They were young, they could expect to remarry, and in the meantime they could move back home with their parents.

Orpah did the prudent thing: kissed Naomi goodbye and went home. But Ruth promised to stay with Naomi forever, to share her house, to worship her God, to love her relatives, to thrive or starve at Naomi's side. That's remarkable enough, for a young widow to throw her lot in with her mother-in-law, but stranger yet is that Ruth was a foreigner to Naomi.

Even though this book in the Bible is called Ruth, it's really the story of how God took care of Naomi. Naomi's bereavement gets mentioned the most often, and at the eventual happy ending of the story, when the neighbors come bringing their best wishes, it's Naomi they congratulate, not Ruth. So Ruth's improbable devotion to Naomi turns out to be the way God saves Naomi from her despair.

It's one of God's favorite ways of blessing us — through the love of our family. Our parents, children, spouses and in-laws support us emotionally, physically, financially and spiritually. And many people outside what we might consider our traditional family can offer us that support. "Family," in God's way of doing things, can include our friends and neighbors, or co-workers; it especially includes our church family, our pastors and brothers and sisters in Christ. When we're sick or otherwise in distress we receive the ministry of doctors and nurses, therapists, social workers and counselors. And we, in turn, minister to the needs of other people in our communities through our careers and our involvement in voluntary services. Maybe the significance of Ruth's being a foreigner in this story is that it forces us to enlarge our picture of who our family is, who it is that we support and are supported by.

The third thing we see in the story of Ruth is faith. But it's an unusual faith. There are no hymns of praise in Ruth, no creeds or professions of belief. In fact, God is hardly mentioned in the story except in casual conversation. Still, the characters and the writer assume that God is reliable, and the way the story unfolds shows that they're right.

When Naomi leaves Moab to return to Bethlehem and urges Ruth and Orpah to stay behind, she prays a blessing for them. "May the Lord deal kindly with you, as you have dealt with the dead and with me. The Lord grant that you may find security, each of you in the house of your husband!" Naomi's prayer creates a climate of expectation in which the rest of the story plays out: and the rest of the way through the book we're waiting to see if Naomi's prayer is going to be answered. As Ruth and Naomi meet with good luck in Bethlehem and put together their new lives piece by piece, we know that God is fulfilling Naomi's hope, even though the writer of the story doesn't feel the need to keep telling us so.

That climate of expectation is faith. Faith is an attitude more than a belief or a doctrine: It's an assumption we carry through life, that God is trustworthy. God is faithful in the big things, keeping his promises to his people, guiding history toward its proper conclusion, but God is also faithful in the small things, dealing kindly with widows, blessing the poor and the lonely.

This lovely little story in the Old Testament is about the blessings of faith, farm and family. In 1984 Sally Field won the best actress Oscar for a movie called *Places in the Heart*, with Danny Glover and John Malkovich. That story is also about faith, farm and family. Sally Field's character, Edna

Spalding, is like Naomi, a widow struggling to make a living on the land in Texas in the 1930s. The bank tries to take her farm, the cotton gin operator tries to cheat her, a tornado nearly kills her and her family. Just as Naomi was supported by her widowed Moabite daughter-in-law, Edna Spalding survives with the help of a couple of unlikely fellow-outcasts: a blind boarder and a black field hand. At the end of the movie all the characters who've appeared in the story, including Edna's late husband and his murderer, are shown sharing holy communion in the little church in the center of town. The scene suggests the heavenly banquet to which God invites us all, and shows that the lives of the characters have been directed by God's love toward a final deliverance.

Now, fate might never deal you the kind of blows it dealt Naomi and Ruth and Edna Spalding, but whatever comes your way in life you can depend on God, as Naomi did, to see you through. God takes care of his people: he blesses us with the things we need to live from day to day. This morning's story reminds us of three of the most important blessings God gives us: a way to make a living, family and friends to love us and support us, and faith to keep us going in expectation that God will continue to bless us.

Proper 27
Ruth 3:1-5; 4:13-17

God's Way
Of Doing Things

I know a couple who have on their wall a framed piece of needlework that someone gave them for a wedding gift. It has their names and their wedding date, and it says, "God gave us each other." I think many Christian couples believe that they were brought together by God's providence. People often feel the same way about their vocations, believing they have been led into a particular life's work by God. As a church, we trust that our plans and decisions are guided by God's spirit.

But why would we think such a thing? How do we know our lives are following any sort of divine intention? God doesn't appear to us in visions and tell us who to marry. I've never known a pastor who claimed to have heard a voice from heaven calling him or her into the ministry. God never serves as a voting member of a church board. Yet we believe God is guiding his people and his church. If that's true, how does it happen?

The story of Ruth tells us about God's way of carrying out his plans, and about how we become aware of God's work in our lives. It's the story of how God saved Naomi from her loneliness and despair, and answered Naomi's prayer for a new home and husband for Ruth.

After the prologue, in which Naomi and her two Moabite daughters-in-law are left widows, Naomi declares herself hopeless, but prays that God will make a new life for Ruth and

Orpah. Things begin to happen in the story after that. Ruth goes home to Bethlehem with Naomi. She goes gleaning barley in Boaz's field, and Boaz takes a fancy to her. Ruth makes a play for Boaz's affection; the only other man with a legal claim to her property renounces it and Ruth and Boaz are married. Nowhere in the story does the narrator says that God has been at work guiding the sequence of events, but at the end of the story you realize that everything that has happened has been part of God's way of answering Naomi's prayer.

So the first thing the story tells us about God's way of doing things is that God is trustworthy. God is faithful to his people, answering prayer, bringing hope where it's needed, giving the gifts that sustain life and make it worth living. As we saw in last week's lesson, Naomi's prayer at the beginning of the story leads us to expect that God is going to act, and even though Naomi might have forgotten her prayer as soon as it was out of her mouth, the expectation creates tension through the rest of the story. Is God going to answer her prayer? Will she be lonely and bitter the rest of her life? Will Ruth marry again? At the end of the story, the tension is resolved: God has listened to Naomi's prayer and restored what had been taken from the two women.

You and I pray to the same God Naomi prayed to, and her story assures us that God listens to our prayers and tends to our needs. We pray this morning for forgiveness, for peace, for healing; for relief of suffering, of poverty, of grief, of loneliness; for solutions to problems in our lives and in our world. And we know that God is working in his own way to answer our prayers.

Ruth's story also tells us that God wields the power to change things. The picture of Naomi and Ruth at the beginning of the story is a picture of sadness, loneliness, poverty and hopelessness. Naomi even tells her friends back home in Bethlehem not to call her Naomi — which means "Pleasant" — anymore, but to call her Mara, which means "Bitter." Yet in the closing verses of the book we see them happy, secure, surrounded by family and friends, celebrating a fresh start in life and the prospect of a glorious future.

The amazing reversal in this story is brought about by God, who is the master of transformation. "See, I am making all things new," God says in Revelation, (21:5) and the goal of God's actions in the book of Ruth seems to be the same as God's goal in the whole Bible: to change something bad into something good. In the beginning God changed chaos into orderly creation. He changed the Israelites' bondage into freedom. He changed death into life when he raised Jesus from the dead. He changes us all from dying sinners into resurrected saints through our baptism into Jesus' resurrection. And he'll change the old corrupt world into a new world at the end of time. We live in a world of sin and death, of frustration and disappointment, but we never need to give up hope for better things. Changing bitterness to joy is God's trademark.

A third thing this story tells us about God's way of doing things is that God's way is full of surprises. What confounded Job in his dealings with God was that God didn't follow the rules of logic or justice. In Ruth, too, God's way is the way of the unlikely. Two childless widows making their own way in life are unlikely heroes of a story like this. Ruth certainly surprised Boaz when she went to the threshing place and crawled into the foot of his bed to convince him to marry her. And the greatest surprise is that this lonely old bachelor and young Moabite widow were the great-grandparents of King David!

Written down at a time in history when the people of Israel were obsessed with maintaining their distinctiveness and their national purity, a story like this — reminding them that their greatest national hero was a descendant of a foreigner — would have shocked them. God shocks us with his choices, too: Israel, his chosen people; Mary, the mother of his Son; a barn in Bethlehem, his Son's birthplace. God doesn't respect race or status or nationality. God doesn't obey rules or pay attention to qualifications, which is good news, because that's what allows God to choose you and me as his children. But it also cautions us to be tolerant, to watch for God in unlikely places and unlikely people.

Finally, this story tells us that God's way of doing things is often a hidden way. At no point in the story is there any obvious sign that God is directing events or guiding people's choices. In fact, the opposite impression is often given: Things appear to happen by random coincidence. Ruth went out to glean in the barley fields, the story says, and "as it happened she came to the part of the field belonging to Boaz." What a lucky break! And Boaz, of course, happened to notice her and find her attractive and hard-working, and Naomi was clever enough to think of a way for Ruth to force Boaz's hand. Luckily, the other kinsman with a right to marry Ruth and inherit the property wasn't interested. So Boaz married Ruth, they had a son, Naomi was happy in her old age, and the family line that was to include King David was preserved. How lucky can you get?

But what appears to be an amazing string of coincidences turns out to be the unfolding of God's plan to take care of Naomi. At the end of the story her friends say, "Blessed be the Lord, who has not left you this day without next-of-kin." If we haven't already realized it as we read the story, now we know that Naomi and Ruth and Boaz have been acting out a script written by God.

We also realize that God works the same way in our lives, and in history. God might guide you in your choice of a spouse and a career, God might lead his church, God might shape the destinies of nations, God might draw the world toward the fulfillment of history, but he does it all from behind the curtain. You are not likely to hear voices or see visions that point out the path for you to take in life. Your life is more likely to unfold the way Ruth's did: through coincidences, chance encounters, the influence of friends and family, doors that open to you here and close to you there.

Now, that can be both comforting and disturbing. It can be comforting because it's nice to know that our lives are in **God's hands, but disturbing because we can't see the pattern,** and we don't know where our lives might be leading.

We also need to be careful that we don't let our faith in God's providence lead us into false assumptions. We can't assume that everything that happens is part of God's plan. We do make mistakes. We are sinners with the freedom to make wrong choices and we do suffer the effects of our sinfulness. God doesn't inflict pain, or reward greed or corruption. Some things happen against God's will.

Nor should we think that we can live our lives passively, waiting to see what will happen next. Notice how Ruth and Naomi worked and planned and schemed to provide for their needs, and only later realized that they were acting according to God's plan. God works through earthly means and human agents, and carries out his work through our choices and actions.

In fact, the only way to see God's work in the world is with hindsight, the way we see it in Ruth. When the story is all told, it becomes evident that it turned out the way God wanted it to. So, how is it that we draw comfort from God's guidance during our lives? By trusting God. Hearing a story like Ruth's assures us that we can trust God to lead us through the twists and turns of our lives until we come out at the right place, even when the way seems hopeless.

That's God's way of doing things, whether he's leading us through difficult choices in life, helping us find ways to serve other people in the world, directing us to solutions for problems in our lives or in our communities, or leading a church in its mission. You won't see God's will announced on a billboard, or in a vision. It might take directions that surprise you; it will certainly change you and the people around you. But it will never fail you. God's way is mysterious, but it's sure.

Proper 28
1 Samuel 1:4-20

Hope For
The Barren

I heard recently about a couple who had tried for years to have a baby — gone to doctors, used all kinds of fertility drugs. Finally, unable to conceive, they had adopted a set of twin baby girls, and when another opportunity came along six months later they adopted a set of twin baby boys, only to discover that the wife was pregnant with triplets.

For couples who want children, childlessness is heartbreaking, and the medical treatment of infertility has become a major industry. The desire to have a baby can become a virtual obsession. Infertility can lead to feelings of disappointment, frustration, guilt, anger and depression.

Hannah knew the frustration of infertility, but she knew much more than that. In Hannah's day, a woman's ability to have children — sons, in particular — was the only measure of her worth. Women were permitted no other ambition than motherhood. A woman who couldn't bear children couldn't turn to her community or career to find fulfillment. She had no reason even to exist.

The Bible often describes childless women as "barren," which is a strong word: barren, like a desert or a dead tree, desolate, lifeless, void, hopeless. Hannah later uses that word of herself. Her life meant nothing, she was worth nothing, all because she couldn't bear a son. Elkanah's other wife,

Peninnah, never let Hannah forget what a joke she was, what a pitiful excuse for a woman.

So Hannah was desperate — desperate for a child, but for more than a child. She needed a sign of her worth, she needed to be shown that she was a real person, that she mattered, that her existence was valid. She needed to become somebody instead of nobody.

When black Americans began demonstrating for integrated buses and lunch counters and drinking fountains in the 1950s, it wasn't just a seat on the bus or a drink of water they needed, it was personhood — recognition that they were whole, worthy human beings. People who look for lodging in homeless shelters need the same thing. More than just a roof over their heads, they need to know that they are not worthless. Hannah felt the same way. She needed a child, but she also needed value and significance as a person. And for that reason, her story is about more than infertility; it's about feeling incomplete, unfulfilled, unworthy and hopeless — something many of us have experienced whether or not we've ever longed for a baby.

So what did Hannah do in her despair? She prayed. With Peninnah's taunts and Elkanah's well-intentioned but ineffective words of comfort pounding her worthlessness into her head, she went to God. She knew she could bare her thoughts and her needs to God without being mocked or condescended to. She trusted God.

"God," she pleaded, "you know how I hurt inside. Don't let me suffer any more. Give me a son! If you do, I will dedicate him to you." It's a surprising prayer, one that you or I would probably not pray. We're uncomfortable with bold, direct, specific prayers like this; we're timid about asking God for what we need. We've been warned against praying selfishly, and against thinking we can tell God what to do, so we don't. Mark Kelso, who played football for the Buffalo Bills in the 1991 Super Bowl, spoke afterward about having prayed when his team's placekicker was attempting the game-winning field goal. (The attempt was unsuccessful and the Bills lost.)

"Looking back I should have prayed for Scott to make it, but I was just praying for God's will to be done."[9]

Of course a field goal in a football game may well be something God couldn't care less about. That's another problem with praying for specific things: choosing silly things to pray about. Ball games, lotteries, the weather on a day we've planned a picnic. Most of us have probably caught ourselves, in a hurry to get somewhere on time, thinking, "O God, please let the light stay green."

But Hannah's prayer wasn't like that. On the one hand, she wasn't timid. She didn't beat around the bush or defer to God's wisdom. She begged God for a son. On the other hand, this wasn't just a prayer for wish fulfillment. What was at stake for Hannah wasn't a football championship or being on time to a meeting or getting rich and famous: she was praying for self-esteem, worth, significance, hope — the very stuff of redemption.

And what about telling God that if he gave her a son she would give him back to God? Wasn't that out of line? It sounds like she was bargaining with God. But I don't think so. I think Hannah's prayer was an expression of her trust in God, part of her constant relationship with God. If God answered her prayer and gave her a son, it must have seemed only natural to her that the son should become part of her response to God.

Hannah understood that prayer isn't a negotiation or a bargain; prayer isn't a technique for getting what we want. Prayer is communion with God, a relationship, a way of life. Prayer is a way of showing that our lives — our hopes, our needs, our gifts — depend on God and are only significant in relation to God.

Hannah understood that, but Eli didn't. He didn't recognize that kind of personal involvement with God. When he saw Hannah standing alone in the temple, crying and pleading silently, he could only assume she was drunk. His first words to her were, "Hey, you, sober up!" This scene was repeated in the New Testament on Pentecost, when the onlookers thought the disciples were drunk when they came out of the upper room filled with the Holy Spirit. People who express their faith candidly and fervently generally seem odd to their more sophisticated, worldly neighbors.

But Eli quickly realized his mistake. He recognized both Hannah's despair and her faith, and his next words to her were a blessing. Through Eli, God assured Hannah that her prayer would be answered. And right away, the story tells us, she went home to eat and she wasn't sad any more.

What a remarkable recovery! Her tears dried up, her appetite came back, the bounce was back in her walk. But why? What had changed? Hannah still didn't have a son. Why was she happy?

She was happy because her greater need had been met. Eli's blessing proved that Hannah mattered to Eli and to God. She was worth something; she was somebody; her relatives and neighbors might have looked down on her, but God didn't. Knowing that God listened to her prayers made all the difference in the world for Hannah. Besides, Eli had given her hope that her more obvious need would be met, too, and God would give her a son. Hannah came to the temple barren — empty, worthless, hopeless — and she walked out filled with hope and filled with grace and filled with the feeling that she was somebody special. No wonder she wasn't sad anymore!

You can have that same assurance this morning. No matter what the world might think about you; no matter what failures you might be carrying around with you; no matter what frustrates you from doing what you think you're supposed to do with your life; no matter what guilt or grief or lack makes you feel like there's no hope for you; you are somebody special to God. God loves you and hears your prayers, and considers you worth the life of his own Son Jesus. There's always reason to hope, because you matter to God.

Finally, in the last verse of the story, we're told that Hannah conceived and bore a son. "Samuel" she named him, because "I have asked him of the Lord." Even her baby's name reflected the process that led Hannah from barrenness to fulfillment. "I have asked him of the Lord." Hannah's dependence on God — her trust, her prayer, her pleading — was the solution to her problem. It was in conversation with God that she discovered her self-worth and her personhood, and in response to her pleading God gave her the son she so desperately wanted.

Hannah was barren no more. She had given birth, she was fulfilled. But her fulfillment had really begun before Samuel came along, when hope was born in her life. When she discovered that God cared about her and listened to her prayer, her life became worth living. Before Samuel was born, Hannah herself was born — began her life as a whole person by the grace of God.

In God's eyes, there are no nobodies. God's love makes us all valid, complete, worthy human beings. Even though we lack things, you and I need never consider ourselves barren, because we can always turn to God and find what truly makes our lives complete.

All Saints' Sunday
Isaiah 25:6-9

What Do We Hope For?

The theme that we hear over and over in these closing Sundays of the church year is hope. Our attention keeps getting drawn to the promised fulfillment of our expectations. God is going to do something to resolve our human predicament, to relieve our despair.

But what is it? What is God going to do? What do we dare hope for?

There was a story in the news not too long ago of a 13-year-old girl dying of a degenerative brain disease. Her doctors wanted to end life-support and let her die, to release her from her unrelievable pain. Her parents refused permission, because they were praying for a miracle. The doctors hoped for a merciful death, the parents hoped for a miraculous cure. Nobody got what they hoped for: the girl died, but her parents' insistence on waiting for a cure prolonged her suffering and denied her a quick end to her pain.[10]

Most of us have shared the joy of members of our congregation who have experienced impressive cures, and the pain of members who have watched hope flicker out. Sometimes instead of a cure we have hoped for spiritual healing, for patience, for courage, for acceptance. What's right? What can we legitimately expect from God? What do we dare hope for?

Do we dare hope for a job when we're unemployed? May we hope for reconciliation in a strained marriage? Can we pray to God about our hopes and plans for our children during the rest of their lives?

We've learned something about hope from our readings in Job this fall. Job hoped for all kinds of things: for physical healing, for an explanation for his suffering, for the return of his good name, for patience. But he never got quite what he asked for. Instead, he got a visit from God, an assurance of God's comforting presence and a stern reminder that what he wanted wasn't necessarily what God wanted.

Today's lesson in Isaiah 25 is about hope, but it's a different kind of hope. Job's hope was for himself, for an end to his own troubles. It was also limited to solutions in this life. Job doesn't seem to have had any vision of a new life, a fresh start, a better existence beyond death, so his only hope was for a reversal of suffering in this world.

But Isaiah's vision shows us hope in its largest dimensions. Isaiah hopes for an end to the suffering of all people, for all times. Isaiah hopes not just for an end to misfortunes but for an end to sorrow itself — even an end to death. Isaiah hopes for a day when all people will be reunited with God and one another and share a great feast to celebrate God's victory. Isaiah hopes for nothing less than a whole new world.

We believe that the new age Isaiah was hoping for has already begun, in the life of Jesus. Jesus called it the kingdom of God — the perfect fulfillment of God's rule. We have all entered that kingdom through our baptism into Christ. Today, on All Saints' Sunday, we celebrate our sainthood, our citizenship in God's kingdom. We celebrate the sainthood of all our fellow believers, past, present and future, and we celebrate our hope for the new age, the great feast of rich food and well-aged wines that God is preparing for us on his mountain.

In Isaiah's vision the new age is inaugurated with a feast. That's understandable — we're entering the time of the year when we celebrate holidays with big feasts. Feasting and banqueting have always been an important form of celebration, especially of family and religious occasions. The Israelites celebrated their deliverance from slavery in Egypt with a Passover feast. The Christian church celebrates deliverance from sin and death with the Lord's supper. Weddings, baptisms and confirmations are usually occasions for feasting. So the Bible often describes the ultimate celebration of the kingdom of God as a feast or a banquet.

One thing that makes feasts enjoyable is the fellowship that banqueters share over their meal. After all, it's the gathering of family and friends around the table that makes Thanksgiving dinner a highlight of the year, more than it is the quantity or variety of food on the table. That's true of the feast Isaiah is hoping for, too. At God's feast all people will be united with one another and with God. Today we are celebrating the "communion of saints," the community of God's people, the family that expects one day to sit down together at God's table for his feast.

One early Christian theologian said the church is like a wheel. All the members of the church are spokes of the wheel, and God is the hub. When you look at a wheel you notice that at the end of the spokes where they get closest to the hub they are also closest to each other. The church is the same way — the closer we get to God, the closer we get to all the other saints who are moving toward union with him. The more intimate our fellowship with each other, the more complete our union with God. At God's heavenly banquet both of those relationships will be perfected.

"On this mountain the Lord of hosts will make for all peoples a feast," Isaiah writes. "He will destroy on this mountain the shroud that is cast over all peoples, the sheet that is spread over all nations. ... The Lord God will wipe away the tears from all faces." All peoples, all nations, all faces. This is a wide open feast. Everyone is invited, not just the chosen few.

I'm sure you've heard the old joke about the new arrival in heaven being given the grand tour. When he passed the hall of praise reserved for Lutherans, he was told to be quiet so they wouldn't hear him, because they thought they were the only ones there. (Of course, depending on who is telling the story, that might be the Baptist hall or the Catholic hall or some other denomination's hall.) Throughout the history of God's dealings with people there have been those who believed God's blessings were only for them, that they would be the only ones in heaven, but Isaiah says that the new world is for all people. Hope is for everyone. In the kingdom of God distinctions don't matter. It's more important to be a citizen of God's kingdom than to be an Israelite, a Lutheran, a Baptist, a Catholic, an American, a bishop, priest or deacon, or anything else.

Well, that all sounds great, doesn't it? A heavenly feast with God and all the saints, a new day when there won't be any death or sorrow or tears. The problem is, we don't see it. Where is it? When is it going to happen?

When Isaiah wrote this passage, God's people had been waiting a long time for God to fulfill his promises to them. We've seen how Job waited and waited for God to answer his cries. The Christian church has been waiting 2,000 years for our Lord to come again. Life, it seems, is more waiting than anything else: waiting for a baby to be born, waiting for Christmas to come, waiting for a doctor to bring life-or-death news, waiting for health to return, waiting for the safe return of a loved one who's far away, waiting to meet the right someone, waiting for our hopes to be realized.

"It will be said on that day," wrote Isaiah, " 'Lo, this is our God; we have waited for him, so that he might save us.' " The life of God's people is a life of waiting, but it's a unique kind of waiting, because we're waiting for a future we have already seen. We've seen the future fulfillment in Isaiah's vision of the heavenly feast. We've had glimpses of the future in the fellowship of the Lord's Supper, which we call a "foretaste of the feast to come," a sample of God's banquet. In the community of Christian people here on earth we've experienced something like the communion of saints in victory. On this day we remember all the saints who have already entered their heavenly celebration, and we see in them an example of the victory that's waiting for us.

Waiting for a future we've already seen, I call hope. May we hope for healing when we're sick? Sure we may. May we hope for companionship when we're lonely? Of course. May we hope for world peace? May we hope for wisdom, for answers to our questions? May we hope for the relief death brings to sufferers? Yes, all those things. But we don't know that we'll receive them. Job showed us that it's possible to hope for the wrong thing and be disappointed.

One hope, though, will not be disappointed. When all earthly hopes die, when all earthly things die, when you and I ourselves die, then there is still the thing we've waited for the longest. Only then, in fact, do we really experience the perfect fulfillment of our hopes. It's the kingdom of God, the final joy that God has promised to all saints. "It will be said on that day, ... 'This is the Lord, for whom we have waited; let us be glad and rejoice in his salvation.' "

Christ The King
2 Samuel 23:1-7

The King
And The Covenant

This is the last Sunday in the church year, and as typically happens at year's end, our attention is drawn in two directions. We look back today at where we have come to arrive at Christ the King Sunday, but we also look ahead into the future — in this case, the ultimate future of a world in God's hands. Over the last eight weeks our first lesson texts have told us stories of hope. We've looked at Job and his journey from hopelessness to confidence in God's wisdom, at Ruth and Naomi and how God delivered them from poverty and despair, at Hannah, who received hope in the form of a son after years of a childless marriage. We've also read from the prophet Isaiah, who brought encouragement to the people of Isaiah when they were oppressed.

Today's first lesson is a reading from the story of King David. In a way David's story naturally follows and sums up the other stories. It displays the same belief that God takes care of his people and provides for their salvation. Besides that, David was the great-grandson of Ruth and Boaz, and Hannah's son Samuel was the prophet who crowned him king.

Yet this text is different from the other texts in this series. In this story, David doesn't receive hope through God's words and actions as Job, Ruth and Hannah did; nor does David announce hopeful news to the Israelites about better times to come, as Isaiah did. In today's lesson David himself is the sign of hope. The life of David became a powerful symbol of hope for the nation of Israel, and the house of David — the line of kings that descended from him — was an enduring sign of God's covenant with his people.

It might seem odd that the Old Testament put such stock in the king of Israel. In our day we're suspicious of the power and character of rulers. We all know the saying, "Power corrupts, and absolute power corrupts absolutely." When we think of an absolute ruler we're likely to think of such recent examples as Ceausescu, Qaddafi, Saddam Hussein or Castro. In nations like Britain, the monarchy remains tolerable because the power of the king or queen is limited. In our country, it has become fashionable during the last couple of political decades to think of government as the scourge of the people rather than as a force for salvation.

The Israelites felt ambivalence about the monarchy, too. Many of them had resisted the movement to crown a king, and the first king — Saul — had been a mixed blessing at best. But David was different. He was devout. He kept the worship of God at the center of the people's national identity. He was wise and just. Most important, he made Israel a mighty nation, just as God had promised it would be. David took a bunch of semi-settled tribes and united them, and then finished their conquest of the Promised Land.

Surely, it seemed to the Israelites, David was sent by God to fulfill his promise. The reign of such a king, our text says, was "like the light of morning, like the sun rising on a cloudless morning, gleaming from the rain on the grassy land." It showed that God directed world events. It also showed that God kept his word, and that God valued honesty and justice. Those two implications of David's rule — that God guided history according to his own will, and that God was just and faithful — filled the people with confidence.

It's hard not to envy those folks, isn't it? Wouldn't it be refreshing to be governed by someone who saw his or her office as an extension of God's mercy and justice, who always represented the interests of the people who most needed representation, who did the right thing without regard to personal consequences, whose every act gave us hope? Instead, office holders and office seekers in our nation seem more likely to view political office as an extension of their personal ambition, to represent the interests of the people who can do them the most good, to do what they think will make them popular, without regard to the long-term good of the community. Our politicians try to win our support by making us afraid of what will happen if we don't support them, rather than by offering us an honest hope for a better society. It's hard to imagine any of our leaders being compared to the sun rising on a cloudless morning after a refreshing rain on the grassy land, except in their own campaign speeches.

Come to think of it, King David wasn't perfect either. He suffered some famous lapses in both his political and his moral judgment. But his reign created a vision for his people, an idea of what was possible, an image of an ideal king who would rule in perfect justice and godliness. And it served as an important symbol and rallying point for the people of Israel. From David's day onward, the Israelites' hope for the fulfillment of God's promises to them centered around the figure of the king who would preserve and perfect the heritage of David.

That's what today's text refers to when it says God has made an everlasting covenant with the house of David. As long as a descendant of David sat on the throne of Israel, the people had proof that God kept his promise not only to the king, but to all his people. The king was the sign of the covenant.

The flaw in that symbolism was that the monarchy didn't last forever. The kingdom split and eventually fell, and the dynasty of David disappeared. Yet, the vision of the ideal king who would fulfill God's promises never faded, and the people began to hope all the more fervently for the day when that king would come to them. If God truly kept his covenant there would still be another king from David's line, who would be perfect in justice and godliness, and whose reign would last forever.

The Messiah, they called him, the Christ, the anointed one. The longer they waited the more they came to realize that he would be a different sort of king, a king whose throne was in heaven and who would defeat not only Israel's Canaanite enemies but all the forces of evil.

The good news for us today, of course, is that the king has come. God's anointed one has been crowned, and has become the proof and sign of God's covenant with his people. The new king was a descendant of David and was born in David's hometown, Bethlehem. Astrologers saw his royal sign in the stars, crowds of people hailed him as the son of David, Simon Peter announced him as the Christ, Mark wrote the story of his life, calling it "the beginning of the gospel of Jesus Christ, the Son of God."

Jesus Christ is the ideal king who carries on God's covenant with his people. When the monarchy of Israel disappeared from history, God's promise didn't disappear with it. It was transformed, enlarged, renewed, extended to the whole world. In our second lesson today in Hebrews 12 we're told that just as David conquered Mount Zion and made Jerusalem his capital, Jesus brings us to the Mount Zion of the living God, the heavenly Jerusalem; and just as David was the sign of God's covenant with Israel, Jesus brings a new covenant.

Jesus, talking about resurrection, used the image of a seed, which is put in the ground and dies only to sprout up as a wonderful new living thing. What is true for individuals because of Jesus' resurrection is true for the whole universe because of Jesus' rule as king: The earthly dynasty of David has been restored as the heavenly kingdom of Christ.

And the reign of our king confirms for us what David's rule meant to the people of Israel. First, it assures us that God is in control of events in history. Nothing can stop God from accomplishing what he sets out to accomplish — not the failings of any earthly kings, not the fall of Israel, not even the death of his new anointed one on a cross. God gave Job and Ruth the same assurance: that no matter what frustrations worldly events might throw in the way, we can depend on

God to bring our lives — and world history — to a destination of his own choosing.

But the heavenly triumph of Christ our king adds something to that assurance. For Job, Ruth, Hannah and David the only hope for redemption lay in this life. Suffering and need that were not relieved in the present age were simply unrelieved. Isaiah announced that there was a better world to come in which all grief would be transformed into joy, and Jesus brought that world into being.

The other thing David's dynasty guaranteed to the Israelites was God's justice. In an ideal nation with an ideal king, good would always overcome evil, the strong would help the weak, the innocent wouldn't suffer, everyone would be provided for. Job questioned God's justice but never stopped believing in it; David's rise to power and Israel's victory over its enemies seemed to reconfirm God's justice, but didn't last. Now, though, we can be certain that God is a just God, and the king who rules in God's name is a just king. God's enemies can't defeat God or us; the people of God will enjoy the fruits of their faithfulness. In Jesus absolute power is made absolutely incorruptible.

The closing chapters of Revelation — the final words of hope in the Bible — tell of Christ's triumph, describing him as King of kings and Lord of lords, and as the Lamb that sits on the throne with God. (Revelation 7:17; 19:16; 22:1) We may take hope from God's promises to us, we may trust that God knows what he is doing, we may believe that our lives will work out the way God wants them to, we may rejoice that God hears our prayers, we may look forward to joining God's heavenly banquet. But our final hope — our greatest hope, the guarantee of all our other hopes — is that Jesus Christ, in whose name we are baptized, is the King of kings. That hope is invincible; that hope alone will save us.

Thanksgiving Day
Joel 2:21-27

Bugs

The title of this Thanksgiving sermon is "Bugs." It's a sermon about bugs — in particular, about a biblical response to bugs. That might seem odd to you, but that's exactly what our first lesson in Joel 2 is: a biblical response to bugs. The land of Judah had been overrun by locusts — grasshoppers — and the prophet Joel was called by God to help the people deal with their bug problem.

You and I have bug problems of our own. Some of them have six legs: cockroaches in the kitchen, silverfish in the bathroom, bees in the yard. But some of our bug problems have no legs at all. When something we're doing doesn't work right, we say there are some bugs that need to be worked out. There are specialists who make their living debugging computer programs. When we're irritated or frustrated we say something is bugging us. When someone is suffering an unknown sickness we say they've picked up some kind of bug.

Those bug problems are minor. The bug problem in the book of Joel was major. Locusts by the millions were laying waste the whole country. Every green leaf had been eaten; the sun was blocked out by bugs. The crops were gone, livestock were dying, people were beginning to starve. Like our own country in the Dust Bowl years, Judah was seriously threatened with ruin.

Nor was the threat just to the economy and food supply. The bugs were eating away at the spiritual strength of the people. With no fruit, no grain, no healthy animals, the people had no sacrifices to offer God in the temple. There was no worship any more, the priests had no ministry to perform. And the children of God had to wonder if the whole grasshopper plague had come about because God wasn't taking care of them any more. Life was infested with bugs at its very heart.

Well, then, we're talking today about something more serious than weevils in the Cheerios, aren't we? These are the bugs that tear our lives apart. Economic recession and unemployment are for us a locust plague — the streets of our cities are full of people without money for rent or groceries or clothes for their children; some of you may be facing the same pressures. Environmental degradation, the hole in the ozone layer, toxic wastes in our drinking water — those are bugs like Joel had on his mind. Cancer, marriages falling apart, AIDS, Cub Scout-aged children with automatic weapons, colleges that nobody can afford to go to. The bugs in today's newspaper eat away at our strength and our nerve just like the bugs in the Bible did.

So on Thanksgiving we open the little short book of Joel in the Old Testament to see what God's prophet had to say about bugs.

The first thing Joel said, just before today's lesson, was "Repent!" You'd expect a prophet to say that. "Return to the Lord, your God, for he is gracious and merciful, slow to anger, and abounding in steadfast love." Many churches use these words from Joel's prophecy about bugs as a call to repentance during Lent.

You see, Joel and the Hebrew people of his day saw everything in life as part of their covenant with God. Locusts weren't just a bug problem, but a sign of a deeper problem. Something was wrong between the people and God. And the bad times also reminded the people of an even greater crisis that was waiting for them come judgment day, the Day of the Lord. God sent locusts to shake the people up, to shock them back onto the right track so they wouldn't get completely lost.

We today aren't as quick as Joel was to interpret misfortune as a punishment from God, but we still need the call to repent. We create many of our bugs by our own indiscretions — ecological, economic, medical, marital — and the suffering they bring us reveals that we need to change our ways. And in a more general way, the fact that we experience miseries at all reminds us of our fallenness, our brokenness, our sinfulness.

The Thanksgiving holiday preserves a tradition that dates back to the Puritan colonists of our country. They had another tradition, however, that we might need to remember as well. Like Joel, the Pilgrims and their descendants called for a day of repentance whenever disaster struck. They understood that the breakdowns in our lives are signs of a much more basic brokenness.

But all of that only leads us up to our Thanksgiving text. After Joel calls the people to worship and repent, he has some great news. "Do not fear, O soil; be glad and rejoice, for the Lord has done great things! Do not fear, you animals of the field, for the pastures of the wilderness are green." "Hey, there's green grass growing, buds on the trees, grapes on the vines and I don't hear any buzzing." It sounds like a pesticide ad in a farm magazine: no more bugs.

That was good news for a couple of reasons. First, of course, it meant that the people would get their livelihood back and have food on their tables again. The nation was saved. But more than that, it meant that God still cared. The people had drifted and doubted, but God was still taking care of them.

We can trust God to take care of us, too, even when we're plagued by bugs. Martin Luther wrote, in his *Small Catechism*, that God "provides me with food and clothing, home and family, daily work, and all that I need from day to day. God also protects me in time of danger and guards me from every evil."[11] God won't let the bugs destroy us; he has both the power and the will to save us from them.

Which is not to say, though, that God is the big heavenly Orkin man. God's providence isn't a technology that will save us when we pick up the phone and call; God's ways are more subtle and more baffling than that. We can't presume on God to solve all our problems for us.

But we can be confident of two things. God is the master of the universe. He created locusts and mosquitoes as well as people and nations and churches and economies and families, and rules over all of them. Besides that, we can be sure that God is for us. The memory of all the things God has done for his people throughout history — especially the gift of his Son Jesus — assures us that God is on our side, blessing us and saving us.

That's what it's all about in the end: God and us. Listen to how Joel ends the passage that is our text tonight. "You shall know that I am in the midst of Israel, and that I, the Lord, am your God and there is no other." The whole point of the bug episode and God's dramatic rescue of his people from the plague, Joel says, is to remind them of their covenant with God. God wants them to remember him, to be aware of his presence, to give him credit for their blessings, to worship him.

And isn't that what Thanksgiving is about, too? Sure, it's a day to count our blessings, to enjoy our families and to help people who have few blessings to count, but it's mainly a day for us to remember God, to be aware of his presence, to give him credit, to worship him.

Thanksgiving can easily become a time for self-congratulation, for celebrating our wealth and successes under the pretense of giving thanks for them. Or it can be a time when we trivialize the problems in the world and the burdens in our own lives so we can feel more like being thankful. But real thanksgiving doesn't rise out of appreciation for the good things we've gotten, or out of ignoring the sorrowful things we've seen. Real thanksgiving rises out of knowing the depths of God's faithfulness to us.

The *Lutheran* magazine recently mentioned words spoken on his deathbed by Archbishop Matulis of Latvia.

> Three times the war passed over Latvia, killing two-fifths of our people. They burned down my church and destroyed the Bibles and hymnals. They took away my wife and I never saw her again. When it was all gone, I realized that I had nothing else in this world but Jesus Christ. It was like a breath of freedom.[12]

Archbishop Matulis had bug problems of biblical proportions. But he also knew the meaning of Thanksgiving — that in the midst of his bugs, he had Jesus.

Today we give thanks for abundance, good health, our nation, our families and all our other blessings. But we also acknowledge the bugs in our lives, that might make it difficult for us to give thanks. Joel — the bug prophet — tells us we can still give thanks: first because God is always working to do away with our bugs, but especially because God is in our midst. He is our God and there is no other.

Notes

[1] "Let Us Prey: False Prophets Con Believers," *Consumer's Research* 72 (October 1989), pp. 17-19.

[2] *The Cost of Discipleship*, revised edition (New York: The Macmillan Company, 1963), p. 99.

[3] *The Atlanta Constitution,* 17 September 1991, p. F6.

[4] *Luther's Works* vol. 54, *Table Talk,* ed. and trans. G. Tappert (Philadelphia: Fortress Press, 1967), p. 52.

[5] Morris Jastrow, *The Book of Job* (Philadelphia: J. B. Lippincott & Co., 1920), p. 28. Quoted in Samuel Terrien, *Job: The Poet of Existence* (New York: the Bobbs-Merrill Co., Inc., 1957), p. 15.

[6] Archibald MacLeish, *J.B.: A Play in Verse* (Boston: Houghton Mifflin Company, 1958), pp. 143-44. Copyright (c) 1956, 1957, 1958 by Archibald MacLeish. Copyright (c) renewed 1986 by William H. MacLeish and Mary H. Grimm. Reprinted by permission of Houghton Mifflin Co. All rights reserved.

[7] John Denver, "All of My Memories," copyright 1971 Cherry Lane Music Co.

[8] Martin Luther, *The Small Catechism* (Minneapolis: Augsburg Publishing House, 1960), p. 19.

[9] Terence Moore, "New NFL front four: Matthew, Mark, Luke, John," *The Atlanta Journal and Constitution,* 25 January 1992, p. D5.

[10] *The Atlanta Journal and Constitution,* 26 October 1991, p. B1.

[11] *The Small Catechism,* p. 10.

[12] Edgar R. Trexler, "A Fair Balance . . ." *The Lutheran* 4:11 (4 September 1991), p. 50.

Lectionary Preaching After Pentecost

The following index will aid the user of this book in matching the correct Sunday with the appropriate text during Pentecost. All texts in this book are from the series for Lesson One, Common Lectionary. Lutheran and Roman Catholic designations indicate days comparable to Sundays on which Common Lectionary Propers are used.

(Fixed dates do not pertain to Lutheran Lectionary)

Fixed Date Lectionaries *Common and Roman Catholic*	Lutheran Lectionary *Lutheran*
The Day of Pentecost	The Day of Pentecost
The Holy Trinity	The Holy Trinity
May 29-June 4 — Proper 4, Ordinary Time 9	Pentecost 2
June 5-11 — Proper 5, Ordinary Time 10	Pentecost 3
June 12-18 — Proper 6, Ordinary Time 11	Pentecost 4
June 19-25 — Proper 7, Ordinary Time 12	Pentecost 5
June 26-July 2 — Proper 8, Ordinary Time 13	Pentecost 6
July 3-9 — Proper 9, Ordinary Time 14	Pentecost 7
July 10-16 — Proper 10, Ordinary Time 15	Pentecost 8
July 17-23 — Proper 11, Ordinary Time 16	Pentecost 9
July 24-30 — Proper 12, Ordinary Time 17	Pentecost 10
July 31-Aug. 6 — Proper 13, Ordinary Time 18	Pentecost 11
Aug. 7-13 — Proper 14, Ordinary Time 19	Pentecost 12
Aug. 14-20 — Proper 15, Ordinary Time 20	Pentecost 13
Aug. 21-27 — Proper 16, Ordinary Time 21	Pentecost 14
Aug. 28-Sept. 3 — Proper 17, Ordinary Time 22	Pentecost 15
Sept. 4-10 — Proper 18, Ordinary Time 23	Pentecost 16
Sept. 11-17 — Proper 19, Ordinary Time 24	Pentecost 17

Sept. 18-24 — Proper 20, Ordinary Time 25	Pentecost 18
Sept. 25-Oct. 1 — Proper 21, Ordinary Time 26	Pentecost 19
Oct. 2-8 — Proper 22, Ordinary Time 27	Pentecost 20
Oct. 9-15 — Proper 23, Ordinary Time 28	Pentecost 21
Oct. 16-22 — Proper 24, Ordinary Time 29	Pentecost 22
Oct. 23-29 — Proper 25, Ordinary Time 30	Pentecost 23
Oct. 30-Nov. 5 — Proper 26, Ordinary Time 31	Pentecost 24
Nov. 6-12 — Proper 27, Ordinary Time 32	Pentecost 25
Nov. 13-19 — Proper 28, Ordinary Time 33	Pentecost 26 Pentecost 27
Nov. 20-26 — Christ the King	Christ the King

Reformation Day (or last Sunday in October) is October 31 (Common, Lutheran)

All Saints' Day (or first Sunday in November) is November 1 (Common, Lutheran, Roman Catholic)

Books In This Cycle B Series

Gospel Set

Christmas Is A Quantum Leap
Sermons For Advent, Christmas And Epiphany
Glenn Schoonover

From Dusk To Dawn
Sermons For Lent And Easter
C. Michael Mills

The Spirit's Tether
Sermons For Pentecost (First Third)
Leonard H. Budd

Assayings: Theological Faith Testings
Sermons For Pentecost (Middle Third)
Robert L. Salzgeber

Spectators Or Sentinels?
Sermons For Pentecost (Last Third)
Arthur H. Kolsti

First Lesson Set

Why Don't You Send Somebody?
Sermons For Advent, Christmas And Epiphany
Frederick C. Edwards

The Power To Change
Sermons For Lent And Easter
Durwood L. Buchheim

The Way Of The King
Sermons For Pentecost (First Third)
Charles Curley

The Beginning Of Wisdom
Sermons For Pentecost (Middle Third)
Sue Anne Steffey Morrow

Daring To Hope
Sermons For Pentecost (Last Third)
John P. Rossing

www.ingramcontent.com/pod-product-compliance
Lightning Source LLC
Chambersburg PA
CBHW060852050426
42453CB00008B/960